DREAM WEAVER

BY

ANNAMARIE VICKERS-SKIDMORE

ISBN: 978-0-244-94188-8

Hi guys, so welcome to book number eight, thank you once again for all your support with my writing. Really hope you enjoy this book and can relate to many of the poems. This book was quite an emotional rollercoaster to write but I'm very proud of the outcome. It is split into three sections Fierce Passion, Love Lost and Eternal Hope, pretty much the recipe for life. Hope you enjoy the ride with me □

Best Wishes as Always
Annamarie Vickers-Skidmore

FIERCE PASSION

MAGNETIC ATTRACTION

After all these years my heart still skips a beat,
Our magnetic attraction sweeps me off my
feet.
There's no safer place than here in your arms,
I became a victim of your disarming charms.

How can your smile chase away the dark?
You devoured my soul and left your mark.
Nothing to fear now that you are mine,
Two fragile hearts now intertwined.

We struggle and fight, sometimes repel,
But always connect as I'm under your spell.
Though time seems to move us further apart,
Nothing can erase your hold on my heart.

We'll shape this world as we desire,
You hold the matches to ignite my fire.
I still believe you're some kind of miracle,
Ours is a chemistry raw and physical.

FORCE OF NATURE

Swept up in a whirlwind of unspoken desire,
Your proximity sets my heart aracing,
With every breath I'm falling deeper,
Enticed by the thrill of tornado chasing.

A tidal wave of mixed emotions,
Threatens to send the heart asunder,
Power that cannot be harnessed,
Reverberates like the sound of thunder.

Chemistry that won't be denied,
A simple touch and sparks appear,
Effective as a strike of lightning,
A heady aroma of passion and fear.

Drowning in azure blue eyes,
Feel my knees go completely weak,
Your caress will lead to my destruction,
But lasting excitement is what I seek.

The first time you stroked my face,
The ground beneath my feet did shake,
Carried away on a wave of love,
My heart has always been yours to break.

A magnetism that's electrifying,
Two souls on a cosmic collision course,
No choice to surrender to human nature,
I lay down my defenses...I'm yours.

UNDER YOUR UMBRELLA

I long to be locked in your embrace,
Your palm placed at the small of my back,
Seducing me with your poise and grace,
As the Summer's day fades into black.

To feel your heart beat so close to mine,
And watch the sunrise across your face,
Your laughter is like the sweetest wine,
Intoxicating leather on lace.

Your eyes sparkle within the moonlight,
Drawing me in till I can't let go,
For your love I would forever fight,
But sadly dear you will never know.

I'll be waiting in the pouring rain,
Hoping that you'll take away my pain.

ROAD TO HEAVEN

Out on the windy moors is a road straight to heaven, where the asphalt simply grazes the sky. To the blooming Heather and cliffs, I lost my heart, my soul chose that moment to be free and fly. Wide open space for miles around, the perfect place to conjure dreams, one wrong turn and pure perfection bathed in sunlight the tarmac gleams. The engine roars and the winds in my hair our journey never quite complete. But we'll keep on riding that road to heaven, to the intersection where sky and road meet.

GROWING PAINS

Gently I hold her hand in mine,
Feel her breath against my cheek,
Her innocent touch feels so divine,
Without her love then I am weak.

Feel her breath against my cheek,
Before she gently kisses my lips,
Without her love I am weak,
Tingles in my fingertips.

Before she gently kisses my lips,
Electricity within my veins,
Tingles in my fingertips,
Linger on like growing pains.

Electricity within my veins,
Your image captured in my heart,
Linger on like growing pains
Whenever I think of us apart.

Your image captured in my heart,
So easy for me to cross that line,
Whenever I think of us apart,
You gently hold your hand in mine.

PARTNER'S IN CRIME

You leave me breathless, Knees all a quiver
Tongue tied, heart racing all in a blither.
Just a midlife crisis, this cannot be love,
You swooped in like an angel sent from above.

For so long I've been building a solid wall,
But you broke through the cracks and watched
it fall.
If I just hold back, my heart will be safe,
I can't be seduced like a small timid waif.

I've carved my compartment, In the tornado of
life,
Its peaceful here no worries or strife,
Far away from any hurt and trouble.
Locked away in my airtight Bubble.

But you sent me freewheeling, ultimate
healing,
Sent my heart soaring right to the ceiling,
Now nothing I do can turn the hands of time,
Two souls, one destiny, intertwined.

CONSTANT CRAVING

There is no immediate fix for a broken heart. What I would give for a syringe of a second chance. A small tablet with the potential to erase punishing words. A miracle drug that would bring you back to my open arms. I would gladly endure the pain if it meant I could hold you again. I'd inject your love deep into my veins as you've always been under my skin. From the moment we collided and watched a nuclear reaction begin. I crave the electricity every time we touch, but somehow my heroin was never quite enough.

SPARK TO A FLAME

I'm a blazing inferno that you cannot tame,
There's a fire in my heart that continues to burn,
Like a phoenix I'll rise when you put out my flame.

I will not come running when you abuse my name,
From my many mistakes I am prepared to learn,
I'm a blazing inferno that you cannot tame.

You made me feel that I am completely to blame,
But I'll be standing tall ready to take my turn,
Like a phoenix I'll rise when you put out my flame.

For letting you into my heart I'll feel no shame,
You tore down my defenses, for love I still yearn,
I'm a blazing inferno that you cannot tame.

So very different yet still one and the same,
For many years you were the rudder to my stern,
Like a phoenix I'll rise when you put out my flame.

No more will I be a part of your wicked game,
From the darkness and destruction I'll now adjourn,
I'm a blazing inferno that you cannot tame,
Like a phoenix I'll rise when you put out my flame.

FINAL CURTAIN

You promised me forever,
I'm guarded and on offence,
I dreamt of us together,
It was only false pretense.

You stole my soul completely,
Gave my sad heart a kick-start,
Caressed my cheek so sweetly,
After tearing us apart.

What happened to perfection?
Soft kisses in the twilight,
Left with hurt and rejection,
Thought sacred vows were airtight.

Put on a great production,
Now I will leave you never,
Heading for self-destruction,
You promised me forever.

DOUBLE TAP

These boots were made for dancing,
Double tapping across the floor,
I'll spin in circles around you,
You'll be running for the door.

I'm the life and soul of the party,
In a pair of killer heels,
I'll step on your toes, no conscience,
You'll know how rejection feels.

You chose to do the walking,
You think I want you back?
Think again my darling,
Tonight I'm on the attack.

My hips will be sashaying,
I'll leave your body shaking,
Tonight I'll be coyly smiling,
And your cold heart will be breaking.

LUCIFER'S FLAME

She crouches low prepared to pounce,
A silhouette against the crimson moon,
Creeping stealthily through the undergrowth,
A huntress humming the devil's tune.

Beauty shining in the darkest night,
She'll have no mercy as the time is near,
Revenge is her only motivation,
Electricity crackles from pure raw fear.

A seductress of both leather and lace,
Her whiplash tongue fires up your senses,
Nowhere to hide from the sultry siren,
She'll incinerate all your defenses.

Once she's caught you in her toxic web,
There's no escaping Lucifer's flame,
The fiery harlot takes her prize,
Another lost soul for her to claim.

Satisfaction has been received,
Until another lonesome night,
When from the shadows a vixen appears,
To maim you with her lustful bite.

APOCALYPSE

Lock your doors and shut the windows tight,
Good and evil wage a war tonight,
Who will win this ultimate battle?
Pure fear will cause your bones to rattle.

Where shadows meet the sapphire lake,
The spirits will find their souls to take,
A candle's flame keeps ghosts at bay,
We all have sins they wish us to pay.

Who finally gets to decide our fate?
All depends on which side you wish to take.
The wheel of life in eternal freeze,
A continuous cycle made to tease.

So on the night when this war is fought,
Take the time to give this idea a thought,
If evil was able to take a stand,
We'd forfeit our passage to the promised land.

LOVE LOST

ALL THAT GLITTERS

A glitter of starlight in the sky above,
Light years away till I feel your love,
Beyond the clouds you’re an open book,
But you turn the page 'fore there's time to look.

There's hurt reflected in your eyes,
Caused by too many little white lies,
I long to take that pain away,
But you belong to night and I to day.

The shadows became your greatest friend,
A beacon I shone brightly till the end,
Just had to choose to walk away,
I lost the fight...now there's nothing to say.

A glitter of starlight in the sky above,
Eclipsed when darkness stole away your love,
I hope one day your spark will return,
All that glitters will not burn.

A SOLITARY TEAR

Just a shimmer in your sapphire eye,
A telltale sign you cannot hide,
You think I'm weakness but I make you strong,
Down your porcelain cheek I will slide.

Cannot hold me back forever,
Soon the dam will overflow,
I see you smile, push me away,
Never to let your feelings show.

You exude power raw and strong,
But everyone must choose to break,
Give into overwhelming emotions,
There's only so much you can take.

I promise you will feel better,
Still be standing after the flood,
Open your heart and let me out,
A solitary tear is understood.

NO MAN'S LAND

Just walk away, don't say goodbye,
You'll never see the tears I cry.
You caused my splintered heart to break,
There's nothing left for you to take.

Emotions scattered on the floor,
Mind and soul constantly at war,
Tentatively reaching for your hand,
Trying to bridge this no man's land.

Words of hurt hang in the air,
Weapons fired without due care,
Wounds appear that cannot heal,
Head whirling like a spinning wheel.

So easy just to take you back,
And Blame myself for all I lack,
But time has stolen love away,
There are no lines to make you stay.

HEAVY HEART

I am just so tired,
My brain is hotwired,
Thoughts move at the speed of light.
Trying to hold on,
Till the pain has gone,
Scared that I'm losing the fight.

My heart is heavy,
Feeling unsteady,
Not sure where to go from here.
I want to be free,
Of your hold on me,
But I cry a silent tear.

There must be a way,
To face a new day,
Without sorrow in my heart.
I'll put on a grin,
And wear a thick skin,
Pretend I'm not torn apart.

CEASE FIRE

There's this cataclysmic void where my hearts supposed to be,
No longer feel the pain, a poor illusion is all I see.

I barely registered the words that brought me to my knees,
Was I just a play thing? A toy to torment and tease?

I thought I was your friend, in the name of misguided youth,
You tore down my defenses and helped me face the truth.

It may sound like a cliché, but you have to love yourself,
Self-belief comes from deep inside, not popularity or wealth.

I'm ready to fight my demons and stare them right in the face,
In this new chapter of my life, they simply have no place.

I'm dispensing of my armour, laying down my shield,
A heart open to opportunity is the weapon that I wield.

LONE SHADOW

I stand alone although you're near,
Wishing that I could disappear,
A big smile painted on my face,
Not a single hair out of place,
Implied confidence hides the fear.

Now everything is crystal clear,
I must not shed a single tear,
You tell me we will run this race.
I stand alone.

Although you see me I'm not here,
Content with bringing up the rear,
Watch me vanish without a trace,
Just one more missing person's case,
Don't miss me when I'm gone my dear.
I stand alone.

FLYING INTERGALACTIC

Far across the galaxy,
Amongst the twinkling stars,
You'll find a blood red planet,
Commonly known as Mars.

We visited the other day,
And skipped across the moon,
Played hop scotch in the craters,
Whilst humming a lunar tune.

The journey was amazing,
Saw comets zooming by,
Streaks of fiery stardust,
Lighting up the sky.

I even made a friend,
A glob of emerald goo,
He introduced himself,
"Hello and how'd you do!"

We nattered on for hours!
He told me quite a tale,
Promised to stay in touch,
With postcards in the mail.

I'll never forget my time,
Flying intergalactic,
I guess it's time to go Home now,
But it really was fantastic!

CIRCLE THE DRAIN

I tried so hard to make you see,
The night that you had left your mark,
You lied and said you needed me,
A light to chase away the dark.
But when the clouds came rolling in,
You took your shelter from the storm,
Again the air was paper thin,
One look and you showed your true form.
You left me standing in the rain,
I knew the scars were just too deep,
Bereft our love flowed down the drain,
A few tears still for me to weep.
I pray one day our sky will clear,
You'll say I am your atmosphere.

LABYRINTH

A never-ending spiral snares me in a vice like grip, Threatens to consume me and tear me apart, Though it feels like I'm slipping further from your grasp, You can take nearly all of me but you can't have my heart.

I've built a fortified fortress and I've thrown away the key,
No clear direction within plain sight,
I'm a perfect reflection of who you want me to be,
Look a little deeper you'll see I'm losing the fight.

Life just seems that bit harder to embrace,
I'm the sandcastle that simply washes away,
Feelings running deeper than the oceans,
Crash and burn around me hard and fast.

Like a phoenix once again I will rise,
The labyrinth I've constructed undeniable,
But every heartbreak has an end,
Fragile to the core yet still unbreakable.

AVA

Our bundle of joy wasn't meant to be,
You were taken from us so cruelly.
I'll never hear your angelic voice,
God decided to make that choice.

You were a twinkle in my eye,
Now your star lights up the sky,
Longing to hold your hand in mine,
To share a simple nursery rhyme.

A line on a stick was just the start,
You left your footprint on my heart,
Within the wind I hear your cry,
It wasn't time to say goodbye.

Nobody quite knows what to say,
They try to take this pain away,
They can't see you're here with me,
Part of my soul for eternity.

I was blessed to have a little time,
You had a name but a short lifeline,
On this earth you left your mark,
My guiding light within the dark.

Now I find my peace up high above,
A galaxy of eternal love,
Ava you may be far away,
But your memory lives on in every day.

A RARE GLOW

Starlight! Star bright! Your beauty twinkles
through the night,
How can you be so far away? I pray each day
that you will stay.

Give anything to see you smile, or maybe hold
my hand awhile,
But you don't see me standing here, wishing I
could disappear.

Precious memories haunt my mind, Inner
peace is hard to find,
The hourglass is losing sand, Beckoning to the
promised land.

I guess it's time for you to know, that only
when I see your glow,
On angel's wings a soul will soar, one more
step to heaven's door.

SANCTUARY

Sleep deprived, buried alive, no way to stop
this strong riptide.
Heart now broken, torn wide open, left me
feeling bereft and frozen.

Hold on tight, but try as I might, no way for me
to win this fight.
Spinning head, feeling dread, now there's
nothing to be said.

Glistening tears, for the many years that you
chased away my fears.
Now in the past, wasn't built to last, it all
seemed to happen way too fast.

Young at heart, from the very start, still we lost
and fell apart,
I cling to the memory, however temporary, that
once I was your sanctuary.

NOVEMBER RAIN

My cheek against the window pane,
I wonder do you think of me?
In every drop of November rain,
Is my smile the vision that you see.

A symphony of hopes and dreams,
Sent out into the atmosphere,
Captured by the Autumn leaves,
But all too soon they disappear.

I picture you in the blazing light,
Am I safely held within your heart?
Was there ever a chance I'd win this fight?
Maybe we're meant to be apart.

Illuminations on the horizon,
A wondrous sight that we both see,
But I'm destined to wait here in the dark,
Wondering if you think of me.

ETERNAL

SHINE

It takes great courage to stand out from the
norm,
From a very early age we're obliged to
conform,
'Finding Yourself' is a cliché it seems,
But who are we really? If we sacrifice dreams.

Our individuality should be admired,
The choices that we make will forever be
inspired.
Ugly is a word that is used every day,
But everyone is beautiful in their own way.

Choose to be noticed or blend with the crowd,
But don't lose the chance to stay strong and be
proud.
Greatness is the sum of all we achieve,
Threads of life make up an intricate weave.
Don't allow others to diminish your light,
When life knocks you down, continue to fight,
Just remember when darkness tries to smother
you,
It's your inner radiance that will always shine
through.

A PERFECT NIGHT

I never believed in love at first sight,
Then you casually walked into the room,
Sashayed to the beat, as my heart went boom,
A new beginning from a perfect night.
You chased away the shadows and brought
light,
Your champagne kisses took away my pain,
Sweet promises made in the pouring rain,
A new beginning from a perfect night.
You whispered my name as I held you tight,
We danced until dawn was ready to break,
My heart and soul completely yours to take,
A new beginning from a perfect night.
I never believed in love at first sight,
A new beginning from a perfect night.

NATURAL WONDER

You are the twinkle within my eye,
Ours is a love that will not die.
I'd take the moon out of the sky,
Sprinkle some stardust where you lie.

I'll build a wall to keep you safe,
In my hands, come place your faith.
Ours is a journey full of wonder,
I'll be the lightning to your thunder.

We will easily weather any storm,
Though riptides leave us broken and worn.
Just know that I won't let you drown,
Now turn that stern frown upside down.

I'll cross the ocean to make you smile,
Just to hear your heartbeat for a while.
There's nothing that I wouldn't do,
So I'll simply go on loving you.

DANCING UNDER THE STARS

Loneliness can be all consuming,
The beginning of the darkest void.
No end to the whirlwind of feelings,
Now despair has conquered and destroyed.

But it doesn't have to be that way,
As we are never truly alone.
With a bright celestial audience,
To illuminate the pathway home.

A twinkling to break through the darkness,
When courage and hope seems to be lost.
A surreptitious glance to heaven,
Can permeate through the Winter frost.

Come join me to dance under the stars,
Let the light roll away the thunder.
No one is ever truly alone,
Claim your spotlight of natural wonder.

YOUR HEART SONG

From your love I will never tire,
The way you hold your hand in mine,
Push my senses right to the wire,
Send shivers up and down my spine.

You'll always be the one for me,
From your love I will never tire,
The first and the last that I see,
One touch will set my skin on fire.

Loving whispers lift me higher,
My life begins and ends with you,
From your love I will never tire,
My bond to you is strong and true.

I've found the place where I belong,
You brought me from the murky mire,
I'm the lyrics to your heart song,
From your love I will never tire.

ONE CHANCE

I noticed you first from across the room,
Staring avidly at the hardwood floor,
Scared to stand out from the milling crowd,
Glancing casually at the open door,
Wondering would it be rude to leave soon?

I pray that you will make the choice to stay,
That you'll capture my heart with just one
dance,
With you in my arms I would be so proud,
Please say you'll at least bless me with a
chance,
I will protect you from harm come what may.

With only a smile my heart does take wing,
Oh what I would give for you to be mine,
I'll wait patiently to receive a sign,
Let us see what this evening may bring.

BELONG

Walk tall and hold your head up high,
Don't ever let them see you cry,
They don't deserve your precious tears,
I'll take away your deepest fears.

Show them all that they were wrong,
You've found the place where you belong,
No one left to taunt you now,
So lead the way and take your bow.

Your standing on a precipice,
Waiting for your armistice,
Easy to cower and retreat,
Harder still to take the heat.

I know you have the strength in you,
To do just what you want to do,
Flash your smile and blaze your trail,
Remember this and you won't fail.

CHALK AND CHEESE

Twenty years from the day that we met,
You are the person I couldn't forget,
At show and tell you had me in awe,
We've battled and raged through every war.

I'll make a vow that we'll never part,
You've built a home within my heart,
I hope you know I'll always be here,
Together we'll face our darkest fears.

On you I know I can depend,
For many years you've been my friend,
Once young girls with strong ambition,
Side by side we did transition.

Chalk and cheese we may always be,
But your strength shines through to me,
Precious memories we have made,
A friendship that will never fade.

KNOCKOUT

Stepping to the left,
Isn't always right,
Altering direction,
Can be a personal fight.

Sparring with emotions,
Head is in a spin,
It would be so easy,
To let the haters win.

Round One! She's glaring at me,
Wants to take me down,
I've studied her tactics,
I recognise that frown.

Round Two! An aim to kill,
A heavy weighted heart,
I'm right where she wants me,
Have been from the start.

Round Three! It could be over,
Nowhere left to hide,
But she's missed the impact,
Made by stubborn pride.

There will be no winner,
No reason to submit,
The challenge was accepted,
An inner fire was lit.

Time for the knockout,
But I'll be standing tall,
I refuse to be defeated,
By the mirror on the wall.

SIDELINES

You're far away but standing near,
Wishing that you could disappear,
But I will always comfort you

And when you shed your lonely tear,
Just know that I'll be standing here,
Yes I will always comfort you.

When life's forever shifting gear,
There's nothing left for you to fear,
As I will always comfort you.

I'll be the one that you hold dear,
Diligently bringing up the rear,
I'm always there to comfort you.

SENSELESS

It’s a senseless world we live in, even our children are not safe. No matter how hard we try, the world is a dangerous place. I just can’t comprehend how an innocent child, can become a ward for evil taking countless lives. Is there no more common decency? What happened to respect for fellow man? It makes me so angry to witness such pain and destruction. We all must come together and stop terror in its tracks. Reach out to those who need us and show them they won’t win. They can’t take away our children and expect us to just give in. Our strength is their weakness and love is the key. I hope one day society will realise war is just tragedy. On days like today the world will come together, to say prayers and send wishes to those lost to us forever. I fear that unfortunately we will never live in peace but we'll keep on hoping that terror will decease.

PERFECTION

Perfection is overrated, we must learn from our mistakes. How can we really know love without a little heartache. Emotion is a fragile thing, we can all be easily broken. But the greatest strength comes from forgiveness, from actions, not from words spoken. You hold my heart in the palm of your hand now do with it as you please. You have the power to be my world or bring me to my knees. Life is a set of choices, it's hard to know what's right. I guess you have to take a chance, embrace the grey, not black and white. Don't put me on a pedestal it's only further to fall, it's our little idiosyncrasies that cause us to care at all.

I TOLD YOU I WAS ILL!

Sorry I can't come play today,
Mum says now I have to pay,
For telling lies and tempting fate,
Now I'm in a real state.

Head is banging, bones are cracking,
Happiness has been sent packing,
Covered in a dodgy rash,
Skin all bumpy like corn beef hash.

Do toes grow crooked from odd socks?
What if I have the chicken pox?
Brain is whirling, stomach churning,
Forehead feels like London's Burning.

Throat is dry and hurts like mad,
I swear I've never felt this bad,
Time to take another pill,
See I told you I was ill!

FAIRLY SUPERSTITIOUS

Let me introduce myself the name is Penny Black,
I'd cartwheel down the pavement just to avoid a pesky crack.
See I have an annoying fault that others may find bad,
I'm fairly superstitious and it tends to drive me mad.

I would never cross on the stairs or walk under a ladder,
You think that that's ridiculous? Trust me it gets sadder.
I really have a feeling there's a chance I could be cursed,
My birthdays on the thirteenth, tell me what could be worse.

Every time I find a penny I have to turn it over,
I’ll never go for an interview without my lucky
clover.
Myself and salt do not get on its scattered all
on the floor,
You can’t imagine the cleaning up it really is a
chore.

Can't leave without my lucky pants and a
sixpence in my shoe,
Every bride knows true happiness relies on
something blue.
I guess I could relax sometimes, after all the
world won’t end,
If a mirror shatters what does it matter, as
you'll always be my friend.

DREAM WEAVER

Our story takes place deep in the night,
When the stars above are shining bright.
A flash of gold and a blinding light,
Our goddess of wonder takes to flight.
You've never seen such a wondrous sight,
As she flaps her wings with all her might.

If you look carefully you just might,
See her shadow moving through the night.
What children would give to glimpse a sight,
Of the dream carrier glistening bright.
When imagination must take flight,
Only then will they see the true light.

She tries her best to avoid the light,
Her wings become singed try as she might.
She longs to soar high and take to flight,
Patiently waits to embrace the night.
In the dark her blazing trail burns bright,
Mouths drop in awe at the glorious sight.

Her very existence defies sight,
Easy to think she's a trick of light.
Just a meteorite burning bright,
Deny her beauty? Try as you might.
When morning comes she fades into night,
Waiting once again to take to flight.

All dreamer's wishes must take to flight,
A dream come true is a stunning sight.
Their whispers are carried on the night,
Celestial orbs of glowing light.
Growing in power and you just might
See their radiance vividly bright.

Children that are extremely bright,
Know how to witness this daring flight.
If they can believe with all their might,
They're sure to see the magical sight.
A sudden twinkle of sparkling light,
Briefly illuminating the night.

You just might see her feathers shine bright,
A spark at night as she takes to flight,
Oh what a sight of harmonious light.

CHOIR OF UNITY

Have the courage to sing out loud,
Don't let them see an ounce of fear,
Eliminate darkness with your light,
Let negativity disappear.

Hold your hands up to the sky,
Show the world that you belong,
Let the sun rise in your heart,
Never let them kill your song.

Raise your voice and show them all,
Miss Congeniality wear your crown,
Our differences just make us strong,
We won't allow hate to drag us down.

Forever we are together as one,
A choir of unity now wide awake,
You haven't begun to scratch the surface,
Ours is a bond you cannot break.

LEAP OF FAITH

Welcome to the dark side, sit back and enjoy the ride. Throw away all inhibitions and forget twisted contradictions. Embrace a little freedom grab all chances with an open heart, don't look on this as an ending it's only really the start. Take what life has to offer and remember who you are, cast all fears aside as it's time to raise the bar. Buckle in for the lows and soar along with the highs, lose a little control break all emotional ties. We don't have to have it together, every second of every day. So live life just for the moment and take a leap of faith.

www.ingramcontent.com/pod-product-compliance
Ingram Content Group UK Ltd.
Pitfield, Milton Keynes, MK11 3LW, UK
UKHW020232250726
13967UKWH00001B/321